First
Facts®

Investigating CONTINENTS

NORTH AMERICA

A 4D Book

by Christine Juarez

PEBBLE
a capstone imprint

Download the Capstone app!

- Ask an adult to download the Capstone 4D app.

- Scan the cover and stars inside the book for additional content.

When you scan a spread, you'll find
fun extra stuff to go with this book!
You can also find these things
on the web at www.capstone4D.com
using the password: namerica.27995

First Facts are published by Pebble,
1710 Roe Crest Drive, North Mankato, Minnesota 56003
www.mycapstone.com

Library of Congress Cataloging-in-Publication Data
Library of Congress Cataloging-in-Publication data is available on the Library of Congress website.
ISBN 978-1-5435-2799-5 (library binding)
ISBN 978-1-5435-2805-3 (paperback)
ISBN 978-1-5435-2811-4 (ebook pdf)

Editorial Credits
Cynthia Della-Rovere and Clare Webber, designers; Svetlana Zhurkin, media researcher;
Kathy McColley, production specialist

Photo Credits
Capstone Global Library Ltd, 4, 9; Newscom: Danita Delimont Photography/Russell Gordon, 21 (inset);
Shutterstock: Aleksandar Todorovic, 19, Anton Foltin, 8 (bottom), 17, Art Boardman, 16, Artem Efimov
(pattern), cover (left) and throughout, BGSmith, 8 (top), Christopher Wood, cover (bottom left), cocozero,
cover (middle), dibrova, 7, Eugene R Thieszen, 13, iko, cover (top), John Brueske, 11, Melinda Fawver,
9 (inset), Mirexon, cover (bottom right), back cover, 1, 3, Movie About You, 21 (back), PhotocechCZ, 14,
Volodymyr Burdiak, 15

Printed and bound in the USA.   PA017

Table of Contents

About North America 5

Famous Places 6

Geography 8

Weather 12

Animals 14

Plants 16

People 18

Natural Resources and Products 20

Glossary 22

Read More. 23

Internet Sites 23

Critical Thinking Questions 24

Index 24

ARCTIC OCEAN

CONTINENTS OF THE WORLD

EUROPE

NORTH AMERICA

ATLANTIC OCEAN

AFRICA

PACIFIC OCEAN

EQUATOR

INDIAN OCEAN

SOUTH AMERICA

SOUTHERN OCEAN

ANTARCTICA

ASIA

AUSTRALIA

About North America

The world has seven **continents**. North America is the third largest. It is south of the Arctic and north of the **equator**. The Atlantic Ocean is east of North America. The Pacific Ocean is to the west.

Central America is part of North America. It is a narrow strip of land that joins North and South America.

continent—one of Earth's seven large land masses
equator—an imaginary line around the middle of Earth

Famous Places

North America has some amazing natural landmarks. The Grand Canyon is 277 miles (446 kilometers) long. It is the largest canyon in the world.

Famous buildings are all across North America. In Mexico, the Pyramid of the Sun was built almost 1,000 years ago. The CN Tower in Canada and One World Trade Center in the United States are more **modern** buildings.

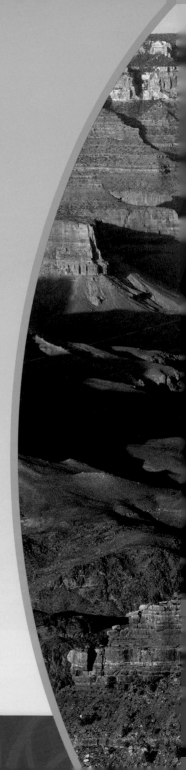

modern—up-to-date or new in style

The Grand Canyon is in the southwest part of the United States.

Geography

Mountains and deserts are found in North America. The Rocky Mountains are in the west. They stretch from Alaska to the southern United States. On the east side of North America are the Appalachian Mountains. The Mojave Desert and the Sonoran Desert are in the southwest.

Fact: Denali is the highest mountain in North America. Its peak is 20,310 feet (6,190 meters) high.

LANDFORMS OF NORTH AMERICA

Denali

Rocky Mountains

Mojave Desert

Sonoran Desert

Appalachian Mountains

A huge area of flat land is in the center of North America. This area is called the Great Plains.

North America also has many lakes and rivers. The five Great Lakes are the continent's biggest lakes. The Missouri, Mississippi, and Rio Grande are major rivers.

Fact: The longest river in North America is the Missouri River. It is 2,341 miles (3,767 km) long.

Lake Superior is the biggest of the five Great Lakes.

Weather

North America has many types of weather. In the south, it is **tropical**. It is hot and rains often. In the far north, it is very cold and there is lots of snow.

Extreme weather can strike North America. Hurricanes form over water. Once on land, they bring heavy rains and strong winds. Tornadoes form over land. They are common in the middle of North America.

A tornado is a giant spinning column of air.

tropical—hot and wet

13

Animals

All kinds of animals live across North America. Polar bears live in the far north. Brown bears live in the forests and mountains in the west. Deer can be found throughout the land. Alligators live in swamps in the southeast. The rain forests in Central America are home to jaguars and countless birds.

jaguar

brown bear

Plants

Plants in North America are very different from one another. In the southwest, a giant plant with spikes grows in the desert. It is a saguaro cactus and can grow 49 feet (15 m) high.

Forests of evergreen trees grow in the north. These trees stay green year-round. Giant redwood trees grow there too. They are the tallest trees in the world.

redwood trees

saguaro cactus

People

People live in 23 different countries in North America. Canada, the United States of America, and Mexico are the biggest. Many of the other countries are islands in the Caribbean Sea. The main languages spoken in North America are English, Spanish, and French.

North America has cities with large **populations.** Some of them are New York City in the United States, Toronto in Canada, and Mexico City in Mexico.

population—the number of people who live in an area

Mexico City, Mexico

Fact: The population of North America is about 565 million people.

Natural Resources and Products

North America has many important **natural resources** and **industries**. Trees are grown in Canada and the United States. The wood is used to make houses and furniture. Oil and gas are mined from under the ground and oceans. Cars are made in many countries. Computers, food products, and construction are other major industries.

Logging is a top industry in Canada.

natural resource—a material from nature that is useful to people
industry—a set of businesses that make a living in the same way

Cars are made in Mexico.

Glossary

continent (KAHN-tuh-nuhnt)—one of Earth's seven large land masses

equator (i-KWAY-tuhr)—an imaginary line around the middle of Earth; it divides the northern and southern halves

industry (IN-duh-stree)—a set of businesses that make a living the same way

modern (MOD-urn)—up-to-date or new in style

natural resource (NACH-ur-uhl REE-sorss)—a material from nature that is useful to people

population (pop-yuh-LAY-shuhn)—the number of people who live in an area

tropical (TRAH-pi-kuhl)—hot and wet; places near the equator are tropical

Read More

Banting, Erinn. *North America*. Exploring Our Seven Continents. New York: AV2 by Weigl, 2018.

Oachs, Emily Rose. *North America*. Discover the Continents. Minneapolis: Bellwether Media, Inc., 2016.

Peterson, Christine. *Learning about North America*. Searchlight Books. Minneapolis: Lerner Publications, 2016

Internet Sites

Use FactHound to find Internet sites related to this book.

Visit *www.facthound.com*

Just type in 9781543527995 and go.

 Super-cool stuff! Check out projects, games and lots more at **www.capstonekids.com**

Critical Thinking Questions

1. Describe one or two natural resources found in North America.

2. Name one animal that lives in the northern parts of North America. What is one animal that lives in Central America?

3. What is one type of weather you may find in North America? Where are you most likely to see that weather?

Index

animals, 14

buildings, 6

Central America, 4, 14

cities, 18

countries, 18, 20

deserts, 8, 16

equator, 5

industries, 20

lakes, 10, 11

landmarks, 6

languages, 18

mountains, 8, 14

natural resources, 20

oceans, 5, 20

plains, 10

plants, 16

people, 18

population, 18

rivers, 10

trees, 16, 20

weather, 12